C000179944

Memories are made of this

31803

Memories are made of this

More British Railways working steam

Mike Esau

• RAILWAY HERITAGE •
from
The NOSTALGIA Collection

First published in 2008

British Library Cataloguing in Publication Data

A catalogue record for this book is available from the British Library.

ISBN 978 1 85794 306 1

Silver Link Publishing Ltd
The Trundle
Ringstead Road
Great Addington
Kettering
Northants NN14 4BW

Tel/Fax: 01536 330588
email: sales@nostalgiacollection.com
Website: www.nostalgiacollection.com

Printed and bound in the Czech Republic

Half title **Weymouth shed: BR Standard '5MT' 4-6-0**
Preparing for the road: driver Peter Miller, based at Weymouth, checks round his Standard 'Class 5' before he backs it down to the station to work a stopping train to Bournemouth. Sadly Peter passed away in 2007.

Page 2 **Farnborough North: 'U' Class 2-6-0 No 31803, 7 November 1964**
The station's canopy and the level crossing set off this picture of the 'U' coasting into Farnborough North with a train for Reading South composed of BR Mark 1 coaches. The bridge that can just be seen in the background carries the main line from Waterloo.

Title page **New Malden: '5MT' 4-6-0 No 73118 *King Leodegrance***
In my first book of photographs published by Silver Link in 2005, *Thanks for the Memory*, I mentioned that before I was married I lived in New Malden. At that time in the late 1950s a steam-hauled train from Basingstoke made a stop at the station at 7.52am, which I was able to use for a non-stop run to Waterloo. Here is the train drawing to a halt in the up main line platform on a rainy morning to pick up a fair number of commuters.

Above left **Near Daresbury, Cheshire: 'WD' 2-8-0**
In the early 1960s my Lambretta scooters gave me the freedom to range far and wide with my camera in the pursuit of steam. My second machine, a TV 175, waits patiently while I photograph the 'WD' plodding uphill towards Frodsham with a hefty train of track panels. The last of these locomotives went out with the end of steam in 1968, but the scooter stayed with me until the year 2000 when I sold it for almost £1,000.

Left **Seaton, Rutland: '2MT' 2-6-2T No 84008**
Later on, with the arrival of our son, the scooter was supplemented by an Austin 1100 car, which can be seen on the left of the picture in the station yard. No 84008 is waiting to leave with a push-and-pull service on the short run to Stamford.

Memories are made of this

Contents

Handborough: 'Grange' 4-6-0 No 6856 *Stowe Grange*
Handborough station had its moment of fame on 30 January 1965 when Sir Winston Churchill's funeral train arrived from Waterloo carrying the body of the statesman for burial at St Martin's Church, Bladon. However, this event was in the future for these local children who seem quite excited by the sight of the 'Grange' scuttling through en route for Oxford.

Introduction

Following up on the success of my first 'Memories' book, *Thanks for the Memory: British Railways Working Steam*, published by Silver Link in 2005, this volume continues the same theme. The book takes its title from the song *Memories are made of this* written in 1955 by Terry Gilkyson, Richard Dehr and Frank Miller, which is always associated with Dean Martin, who recorded a chart-topping version in 1956. This was a year when steam traction was still the norm on Britain's railways, though its days were numbered as forecast in the British Transport Commission's Modernisation Plan published the year before. I hope you will enjoy this new selection of 'memories' as much as I have enjoyed putting them together. They are simply divided into four sections to reflect the diversity and range of working steam in its last ten years or so of its life – 'Main-line action', 'Secondary and cross-country lines', 'Branch lines' and 'Freight workings'.

Nowadays in the world of photography the 'big D' – digital – reigns supreme, modern computer software making it possible to easily manipulate images after the camera shutter is fired – 'tidying up the picture' as it is often known. A well-respected manufacturer's current advertisement on the radio for one of their popular digital SLR cameras perhaps sums the possibilities up by saying 'welcome to the [digital] playground'. All the pictures in this book of course pre-date the digital age so are perhaps what might be termed in modern parlance as 'organic' with no artificial additives or colours – what you see is truly what was there at the time. Mind you, even in steam days some photographers were not averse to an innocent bit of enhancement of a black and white picture in the darkroom, perhaps by printing in some good locomotive exhaust or a striking sky from another negative. However, this took considerable skill to be successful but did not alter the essential elements of the picture.

In general, photography in the working steam era was a much more relaxed activity than it is now, even if the equipment in use was not so sophisticated. A great advantage to the railway photographer was the rich variety of lineside fixtures and fittings still in use, which could add so much to the atmosphere, composition and impact of a picture. I still have a one or two 'steam age' cameras such as a classic Zeiss Super Ikonta. This 6cm x 9cm format camera made in the mid-1950s is a beautiful, tactile though ponderous piece of equipment, the relatively slow pace of its operation being in tune with the time it was made – calculate the exposure with a light meter, set the appropriate shutter speed and lens aperture, make sure the film is wound on, focus the camera using the coupled rangefinder, cock (tension) the shutter, look through the less-than-perfect eye-level viewfinder and finally press the shutter release button at the right time. One shot per train and eight pictures on a film – that was it.

Now, with only comparatively few steam workings, especially on our troubled national network, more and more people wishing to see and photograph them, together with concerns about terrorism and health & safety issues, railway photography can at times be a quite stressful experience! With the rapid rise in availability of good mobile phone cameras, everybody seems to be a photographer these days so the competition for the best vantage point is sometimes quite intense at popular locations. However, in compensation the capabilities of modern digital cameras do allow the maximum potential to be extracted from those opportunities that are offered and allow pictures to be taken that would not have been possible in the 1950s and 1960s, especially with something like my 'hands-on' Super Ikonta. Nevertheless, despite the limitations of such equipment compared with what is available today, I suggest that in those last few years leading up to the end of steam in 1968 steam railway photography reached a level of maturity and excellence that has subsequently not been surpassed.

I know several railway photographers whose flagging interest in the art has been rejuvenated by the opportunities offered by digital SLR cameras, but in my own case I have a comprehensive modern film-based medium-format SLR system that I am loathe to discard at the moment. Probably the time to change will come when I am no longer able to cope with the weight of the cameras and their lenses, quite apart from the possible future difficulty in getting the equipment repaired. But I think photographers today must count themselves lucky in having both film and digital systems at their disposal. Fortunately film and photographic paper and associated items are still readily available, though the number of manufacturers, retail outlets and professional processors is diminishing, especially for transparency film processing. Despite these factors there is something magic in the jewel-like quality of a well-exposed transparency, especially when a number are viewed on a light box, a pleasure that no memory card can offer. Equally a black and white print produced in a darkroom from a good negative is also very satisfying, which will be equal to the day the picture was taken provided the negative has been processed properly and looked after. It has certainly given me a great deal of satisfaction to print the pictures for this book especially where I have been able to improve upon the quality of prints made several years ago.

As with *Thanks for the Memory* I must apologise for not being able to give dates on many of the pictures since I was very lax in making notes at the time. Once again my brother David has come to the rescue with dates for some of the pictures and you will see that he is featured on page 8. 'The two Johns', John Edgington and John Gilks, have as always been a mine of information and very helpful in aiding my none-too-perfect memory when writing the captions, but if there are any errors they are my responsibility. I have also been through the pictures with my long-time friend Dr Gerald (Gerry) Siviour and we have relived some of the many trips we enjoyed in steam days. Once again my wife Alison has also been of great support, not only with suggestions and helpful comments but also as a contributor, for two of her splendid colour pictures are reproduced in the colour section. My black and white versions were unexciting by comparison!

Finally I am indebted to Peter Townsend for giving me the opportunity to present another selection of my pictures and of course to Will Adams and Mick Sanders at Silver Link Publishing who have been of great help to me in producing the book. I am therefore particularly pleased to be able include a photograph of the company's 'A4' 'Pacific' namesake on page 26.

Mike Esau
Richmond, Surrey
2008

Pulford Siding Signal Box: '5MT' 4-6-0 No 45429
As I have mentioned in my Introduction, almost all of the wonderful things that could be seen on the lineside in the steam era have now disappeared and, try as they might, our private railways are not able to recreate a scene such as this. The Class 5 is heading south towards Shrewsbury past Pulford Siding Signal Box some 5 miles south of Chester. What a beautiful little box this is, even with that impossibly tall chimney.

Main-line action

I have arranged the next 30 pages more or less geographically to thus show the wide variety and contrast in the types of locomotives and trains that could still be seen on Britain's main lines in the 1950s and 1960s. Sadly there have been significant losses since the steam era, such as the Midland main line through the Peak District, the Great Central main line and of course the much lamented 'Waverley' route.

Elsewhere the steam-worked express passenger service out of Waterloo to Bournemouth and Weymouth was the last of its type, with the Bulleid 'Pacifics' and BR Standard types running right up to the full commissioning of electrification in July 1967. The Paddington to Birmingham and Wolverhampton line was another notable location, where, as they passed through the Chilterns, 'Kings' and 'Castles' shared the line with one-coach vintage push-and-pull trains worked by Victorian-looking '1400' Class 0-4-2Ts. In the beautiful Golden Valley on the line from Gloucester to Swindon similar contrasts in motive power could be seen, epitomised by the pictures on pages 16 and 17. The classic inside-cylinder 4-4-0 could also still be photographed hard at work right up to the early 1960s – for example, the speedy Maunsell 'D1s' and 'E1s' on front-line workings into Kent, charismatic 'T9s' in Hampshire and the West Country, a few survivors of Great Eastern Railway design in East Anglia, and Fowler 2Ps piloting main-line trains on the London Midland Region and the Scottish Region. There was much variety too with the coaching stock in use, ranging from the new BR Mark 1 designs to old pre-grouping stock as shown in the pictures I took at Slough and Coventry.

Stations were also very different, a world away from the sterile environment we often find today. Perhaps the old order is shown best by the cluttered scene at Birmingham New Street on page 30, wonderful material for the railway photographer, as well as the scene on page 27 of King's Cross softened by drifting smoke and steam, worlds away from the reborn St Pancras of 2007, with its features sharply defined, clean and colourful.

Out on the main line there was so much more than today for photographers to include in their pictures. The diverse features that we then took for granted such as signal boxes, water troughs, attractive rather than prison-like lineside fencing and those impressive lines of telegraph poles and their wires, as seen on page 25, are of great interest today. Of our private railways, only the Great Central Railway in Leicestershire presently has the potential to recreate a true steam-age main line on its double-track section between Loughborough and Rothley. While that railway has achieved a great deal towards this, the reinstatement of the telegraph pole route would be the icing on the cake to really bring back memories of those who experienced the steam-worked main line. Who can forget being in an express as two trains passed at speed – first a 'whoosh' from the locomotive, then the blur of passing coaches and, if it was an important train, a flash of white from the tablecloths in the dining car. Wonderful times!

North of Haddenham: 'King' 4-6-0
Main-line action personified: my brother David and I often used to visit the Paddington to Birmingham line to photograph the 'Kings' on what proved to be their last regular front-line duties. David has told me that he thinks he is not photographing this train because of camera failure, so I probably asked him to complete the picture by standing near the attractive cast-iron signs as the 'King' pounded towards Bicester.

Above **Elm Road level crossing, New Malden: Rebuilt Bulleid 4-6-2**
Quite close to my parental home, my son, who is standing by the phone box, watches a rebuilt Bulleid 'Pacific' speeding towards Waterloo. The level crossing in the foreground is on the line between New Malden and Kingston. As always the cars of the period are now just as interesting as the train.

Below **Wool: Rebuilt 'Merchant Navy' 4-6-2 No 35008 *Orient Line***
These two smartly attired schoolgirls seem unimpressed by the huge bulk of the 'Merchant Navy' on the A352 road level crossing at Wool. A Whitbread beer lorry and a Morris Oxford car also wait to continue their journey east.

Left **Waterloo: 'West Country' 4-6-2 No 34038 *Lynton***
This very dirty 'West Country' enjoys a spot of impromptu cleaning from some spotters at Waterloo, while in the foreground a father explains some finer point of detail to what I imagine is his son. Just look at that impressive cine-camera – I wonder if the film taken with it still exists.

Below **Waterloo: Rebuilt 'West Country' 4-6-2 No 34093 *Saunton***
It's a warm summer evening at Waterloo. *Saunton*, though now without nameplates, is slowly pulling out of the station, closely observed by some enthusiasts. Further up the platform some railway staff are deep in conversation.

Right **Basingstoke: Rebuilt 'Merchant Navy' 4-6-2 No 35013 *Blue Funnel***
Undertaking a job that had to be carried out day and night in all weathers, the crew top up the tender with water at Basingstoke, watched by some members of the platform-end locospotters gallery.

Below **Dorchester South: '4MT' 2-6-0 No 76009**
Further down the line at Dorchester South station the crew of the locomotive, bound for Weymouth, chat with a permanent way man. Maybe some member of the shed staff at Weymouth, with its Great Western connections, thought it would be amusing to blank out the '7' in the locomotive's number so it could try to masquerade as 'King' 4-6-0 No 6009 *King Charles II*!

Above **Earlsfield: 'West Country' 4-6-2 No 34103 *Calstock***
Snow always adds interest to a photograph, but here, towards the end of the hard winter of 1962/63, it is rapidly melting. No 34103 is working the 12.35pm train from Waterloo to Bournemouth. For some reason I took very few pictures at Earlsfield, perhaps because of the greater opportunities at nearby Clapham Junction or Wimbledon. Notice that the signal box nameboard has been removed and is resting on the platform.

Left **Near Ashford (Kent): 'King Arthur' 4-6-0 No 30782 *Sir Brian*, 25 February 1962**
The Locomotive Club of Great Britain's (LCGB) 'Kentish Venturer' railtour ran in some bitter weather. No 30782 has worked the train from Victoria and is approaching Ashford in a snowstorm, having travelled via Chatham and Dover. The cold was accentuated by the failure of the heater in Gerry Siviour's Ford Prefect car, which we used to follow the train down to New Romney.

Right **Honiton Bank: 'West Country' 4-6-2 No 34092 *City of Wells***
It is a miserable wet day on the bank as No 34092 climbs the 1 in 80 gradient towards Honiton Tunnel with a local train from Salisbury to Exeter consisting of three Bulleid coaches.

Below **Axminster: 'West Country' 4-6-2 No 34030 *Watersmeet***
Some 8 miles to the east, *Watersmeet*, on a train to Salisbury, has paused at the station and is taking water. The overbridge frames the picture to perfection.

Left **Meldon Viaduct: 'T9' 4-4-0 No 30338, April 1960**
Riding high above the valley of the West Okement, the 'T9' is working a train bound for Wadebridge and Padstow on the North Cornwall line. This location was a 'must' during any visit to the West Country and, given its location close to Dartmoor, we were lucky to have sunny weather on this occasion. The viaduct was opened in 1874 but closed after the withdrawal of train services west of Okehampton in 1968. However, it still survives and is now part of the 'Granite Way' cycle path.

Below **Near Bodmin Road: 'Grange' 4-6-0 No 6869 *Resolven Grange***
The Penzance to Plymouth line could boast substantial stone viaducts in marked contrast to the spindly structure at Meldon. The 'Grange' is crossing one of the many viaducts on the climb between Bodmin Road and Doublebois with an eastbound train containing five milk tankers. Note the foundations of the earlier Brunel viaduct seen through the nearest arch.

Right **Near Lydford: 'T9' 4-4-0 30715, April 1960**
Southern Region trains between Plymouth and Exeter were very different in character from their Western Region counterparts. It was wonderful to see 'T9s' still on front-line duty as late as 1960. Close to the slopes of Dartmoor, the old 4-4-0 is in charge of the Plymouth portion of the eastbound 'Atlantic Coast Express'. The train will have left the Devon seaport around 10am to arrive at Waterloo some 5½ hours later.

Below **Dainton: ' Manor' 4-6-0 No 7820 *Dinmore Manor* and 'King' 4-6-0 No 6029 *King Edward VIII***
On the Western Region route from Plymouth to Exeter it was all noise and fury as heavy trains struggled over the South Devon banks. Here is the up 'Cornish Riviera Express' composed of a smart rake of chocolate and cream BR Mark 1 coaches, approaching Dainton Tunnel in the summer of 1958.

Ham Mill Crossing: 'Castle' 4-6-0 No 7037 *Swindon*

What a great sight the smartly turned out 'Castle' makes proudly steaming up the Golden Valley past Ham Mill Crossing Halt near Stroud with a train from Gloucester to Paddington. This was a superb stretch of line for photography in steam days and could always be relied upon to produce some memorable pictures.

Right **Brimscombe Bridge Halt: '9400' Class 0-6-0PT No 9453**
The big 0-6-0PT is an unusual choice to work this Gloucester-bound local train, which is crossing the derelict Thames & Severn Canal. The waiting shelter at the Halt looks rather precariously supported by three girders projecting from the retaining wall.

Below **Chalford: '1400' 0-4-2T No 1472**
More usual motive power for the local trains in the Golden Valley were the push-and-pull-fitted '14XX' tank locomotives. In this tranquil scene on a sunny spring day, the locomotive's crew relax on a station seat before the return working to Gloucester. There is a spare auto-coach in the siding.

Above **Southall: 'Hall' 4-6-0 No 5988 *Bostock Hall***
The fine station buildings at Southall form the backdrop to this picture of the 'Hall' passing through on the up relief line with a summer Saturday train bound for the Southern Region via the West London line. In the sidings '6100' Class 2-6-2T No 6169 is marshalling some vans.

Left **Slough: '6100' 2-6-2T No 6122**
Slough is not normally associated with architectural excellence, but there is no doubt about the quality of the station's fine domed roof and ornamental ironwork seen in this picture. The large 2-6-2Ts were the preferred motive power for the local trains to Paddington, such as this one, composed of a London District close-coupled set.

Above **Near Ilmer Halt: '1400' 0-4-2T**
The Western Region ran a push-and-pull service calling at all stations between Princes Risborough and Banbury, which, like this northbound train, took just over an hour for the 33-mile journey. They made an interesting contrast with the expresses to and from Paddington hauled by 'Kings' or 'Castles'.

Below **Near Haddenham: 'King' 4-6-0**
Here is one the expresses to Birmingham crossing a short viaduct over the River Thame just north of Haddenham. Due to electrification work on the Euston line, an hourly service ran between Paddington to Birmingham (Snow Hill), which, as I mentioned on page 8, proved to be something of a swansong for Western Region express steam power. This provided a unrepeatable opportunity for the photographer to depict the 'Kings' in full cry.

Left **Near Clarbeston Road: 'Manor' 4-6-0 No 7815 *Fritwell Manor***
Alison and I spent a very pleasant week in the far west of Wales in the summer of 1963, an area not much frequented by railway photographers in steam days. This pleasing scene shows the 'Manor' heading east with a train consisting of three BR Mark 1 coaches and an insulated fish van behind the locomotive.

Below **Tenby: '5100' Class 2-6-2T**
Further south during the same holiday, a 2-6-2T is leaving Tenby with a local train to Pembroke Dock. The rather unsightly caravan park emphasises the importance of the holiday trade in this area.

Near Charlbury: 'Castle' 4-6-0 No 5025 *Chirk Castle*, 20 October 1962
I spent many happy hours photographing 'Castles' on the Oxford to Worcester line in the early 1960s, the scene of their last regular main-line duties. A train I always tried to see was the all-stations 1.20pm Thursdays-and-Saturdays-only Oxford to Moreton-in-Marsh, which invariably was worked by a 'Castle', perhaps as a 'filling-in' turn. Despite the bent handrail along the side of the boiler, the locomotive makes a beautiful sight drifting along near Charlbury water troughs with this lightweight train.

Left **Camden shed: 'Princess Coronation' 4-6-2 No 46233 *Duchess of Sutherland***
Camden was a cramped and busy shed as I think is shown in this picture of the Edge Hill shed 'Duchess' squeezing under the coaling tower.

Below **Willesden shed: Rebuilt 'Royal Scot' 4-6-0 No 46166 *London Rifle Brigade***
Further up the line at Willesden, the well-proportioned lines of the 'Scot' exude a sense of pent-up power, personified in this portrait of the locomotive resting between duties.

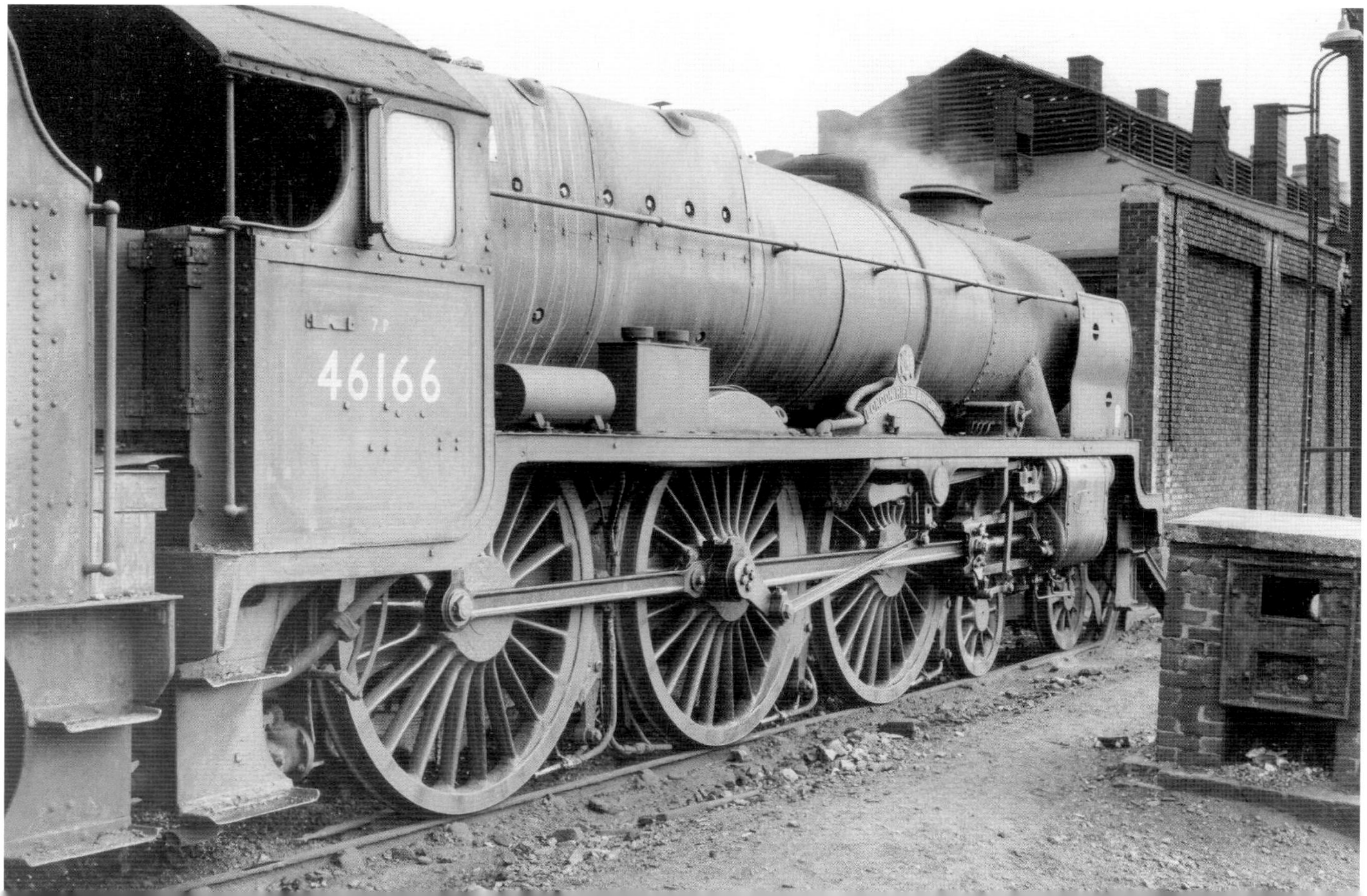

Camden: '8P' 4-6-2 No 71000 *Duke of Gloucester*
This picture was taken during a Railway Correspondence & Travel Society (RCTS) shed visit to Camden in 1962, which was also attended by fellow photographer Mike Pope. We had photographed the locomotive on shed and here it is coming up Camden bank with the 7.10pm 'Northern Irishman' to Stranraer.

South of Berkhamsted: '5MT' 4-6-0 No 45024

Before the advent of electrification and the installation of the overhead catenary, there were some attractive locations where the main line out of Euston ran alongside the Grand Union Canal. Local fishermen seem oblivious to the passage of the 'Class 5' speeding north over the canal at Bourne End.

Above **Near Luton: '6P' 'Jubilee' 4-6-0 No 45622 *Nyasaland*, 4 February 1961**
Because of the time it took to reach the Midland and East Coast main lines from my home on the west side of London, I made far fewer visits to this area than I would have liked. However, I was lucky with the weather on this trip and was impressed by the fine telegraph pole route lining the track of the Midland main line out of St Pancras. Amidst typical rolling Hertfordshire countryside the 'Jubilee' is heading north with an express for Leicester and beyond.

Below **Knebworth: 'A1' 4-6-2 No 60145 *Saint Mungo***
A little way over to the east from the Midland main line the 'A1' makes a pleasing sight as it passes through the station with a train for the north. Domestic coal traffic is very much in evidence in the goods yard.

King's Cross shed: 'A4' 4-6-2 No 60014 *Silver Link* and 'A1' 4-6-2 No 60119 *Patrick Stirling*
Given the name of my publisher, I am pleased to be able to include this photograph of the 'A4' standing outside the shed ready for its next duty. The locomotive has been beautifully cleaned, a total contrast to the adjacent 'A1'. The low viewpoint emphasises the sleek lines of the 'A4'.

King's Cross: 'A1' 4-6-2 No 60144 *King's Courier*; 'A4' 4-6-2s Nos 60026 *Miles Beevor* and 60032 *Gannet*

At the time I was writing this caption, the refurbished St Pancras station had just re-opened. Its clean sparkling interior of 2007 is worlds away from neighbouring King's Cross station on a typically murky day in the late 1950s. In a scene so evocative of the time, a lone enthusiast, well wrapped up against the cold east wind, watches the 'A1' getting 'The West Riding' on the move. Meanwhile three enginemen make their way into the station as No 60032 arrives with an express from the north.

Above **Near Wymondham: '7MT' 'Britannia' 4-6-2 No 70011 *Hotspur***
Gerry Siviour and I are along the lineside early to photograph the 4.36am Liverpool Street to Norwich train, which ran via Cambridge and Ely. The stock is a mixture of Gresley, Thompson and BR Mark 1 coaches together with some vans at the back for mail and parcels.

Left **Colchester: 'B17/6' 4-6-0 No 61663 *Everton***
There was always something a little special about the 'B17s', perhaps because the names they carried gave them some extra glamour, even if they were not as successful as the 'B1s' that they closely resembled. On a dismal wet day in 1958 No 61663 is waiting to leave the station with a train for Clacton.

Right **Newmarket: 'B1' 4-6-0 No 61055**
The 'B1' is coasting into the station with a stopping train for Cambridge.

Below **Cowbit: 'B1' 4-6-0 No 61205, May 1961**
On the busy GN/GE Joint line between Sleaford, Spalding and March, with its procession of freights, this train was most unusual. The 'B1' is hauling a Hastings-gauge Maunsell coach and two old tenders, which may perhaps be carrying water to supply the cottages at the remotely situated crossings along the line.

Left **Birmingham New Street: '7MT' 'Britannia' 4-6-2 No 70044 (later) *Earl Haig* and '6P' 'Jubilee' 4-6-0 No 45670 *Howard of Effingham*, summer 1955** While stationed at RAF Hednesford in 1955 during my National Service, I often visited the Birmingham area with my camera. Amidst the day-to-day clutter of this busy station I was able to photograph one of the two 'Britannias' that were fitted with Westinghouse air brake equipment when outshopped from Crewe Works in 1953. No 70044 and the 'Jubilee' are waiting to leave with trains for the north.

Below **Coventry: '4MT' 2-6-4T No 42428, 11 August 1955** I am on my way home on leave from RAF Hednesford, having just finished my 'square-bashing'. The train to Euston, hauled by No 46135 *The East Lancashire Regiment*, has stopped just in the right place to enable me to take this picture of a local train waiting to leave for Nuneaton from the down platform; it is composed of an ex-Midland Railway close-coupled set of coaches.

Miller's Dale: '4F' 0-6-0 No 44566; '4P' 'Compound' No 41062 and 6P 'Jubilee' No 45628 *Somaliland*
One cold snowy day in the winter of 1958/59 I travelled by train over the 30 miles from Manchester Central to take some pictures around Miller's Dale. The '4F' is trundling through the station on the down slow line, while the 'Compound' and 'Jubilee' have just swept in to stop in the main-line platform. The driver and inspector on the 'Jubilee' look keen to get away for the last section of the journey to Manchester.

Ais Gill: '5MT' 4-6-0 No 45012

My brother and I are on our way to the North East in the summer of 1965 to photograph steam, and have stopped off on the Settle & Carlisle line. The light is superb for us to capture this Carlisle Kingmoor Class 5 putting out a fine display of smoke as it nears the summit with a vans train.

Dillicar troughs: 'Princess Coronation' 4-6-2 No 46233 *Duchess of Sutherland*
This picture has all the elements of a fine day in early summer with a lovely hay meadow in the foreground. The 'Duchess' is making light work of its train of eight coaches and should have no difficulty in climbing Shap a few miles ahead.

Glasgow St Enoch: '2P' 4-4-0 No 40686 and '6P' 'Jubilee' 4-6-0
The mighty twin glass and iron roofs of the station form the backdrop to this picture of the relief to the 'Thames-Clyde Express' leaving the station for the south. The train took the best part of 10 hours to reach St Pancras via Dumfries and the Settle & Carlisle line. The '2P' is displaying a Caledonian Railway-style route indicator at the top of the smokebox.

Right **Hawick: 'K3' 2-6-0 No 61917, 31 July 1961**
My father worked for most of his career for the knitwear firm Peter Scott whose factory was, and still is, in Hawick. I remember arriving with him early one morning off the sleeper from St Pancras, which had been hauled from Carlisle by blue-livered 'A3' No 60035 *Windsor Lad*. It was always a pleasure to go back there again in later years, such as on this occasion when I photographed the 'K3', normally seen on freight workings, on this local train from Edinburgh.

Below **Millerhill: 'B1' 4-6-0 No 61239, 31 July 1961**
The 'B1' has not long turned off the East Coast main line and is heading towards Galashiels and Hawick with a 'Waverley' route stopping train.

Dalwhinnie: '5MT' 4-6-0 No 45473
I am travelling back from Inverness to Perth on my railway holiday to Scotland in 1959 and my train has stopped to allow a heavy northbound service to pass. The two 'Class 5s' are coasting down the 1 in 80 gradient from Druimuachdar summit to stop at the station. Meanwhile the driver of No 45473 looks relaxed puffing his pipe and the feather of steam from his locomotive's safety valves augers well for the stiff climb ahead.

Fort William: '5MT' No 73078; 'J36' 0-6-0 No 65313, summer 1959

I have to admit that the old station at Fort William alongside Loch Linnhe, closed in 1975, was far more photogenic than the new one, as can be appreciated from these pictures. The Standard Class 5 has arrived as the leading locomotive on a train from Glasgow – just seen behind it is 'K2/2' 2-6-0 No 61764 *Loch Arkaig*. At the other end of the station on this fine summer evening the 'J36' is shunting the stock of a train from Mallaig, which includes an ex-LNER observation car.

Secondary and cross-country lines

These lines were equally as interesting as the main arteries of our railway system and displayed an even greater array of motive power, as is shown by the pictures in this section. The Southern Region was still using vintage locomotives well into the 1960s – for example the 'M7', 'H' and 'E4' classes in Kent, Sussex and Surrey, quite apart from the 'O2' 0-4-4Ts in the Isle of Wight – so it was always a delight to go and photograph them. To add to the interest, modern London Midland Region and the Standard classes were beginning to replace the older locomotives on some of the workings, adding to the variety of what could be seen. The picture on page 46 of St Leonard's shed illustrates very well the range of locomotives in use at the time, 70 years separating the building dates of the 'Q1' and 'Terrier'!

Being within easy cycling distance of my home, the scenic cross-country Redhill to Guildford line was always rewarding to visit, especially to see the passage of the heavy through trains between the Midlands and the South Coast. On Christmas Eve 1960 I have a vivid memory of photographing newly overhauled 'N' Class No 31817 as it climbed the 1 in 100 gradient out of Guildford with a heavy train of BR Mark 1 coaches bound for Oxford and the Midlands. I was with Gerry Siviour, who has particular cause to remember the occasion. We took the picture from the A3 road bridge, where, unlike today, it was still possible to photograph trains, but Gerry had to park the car safely. By the time he had done so he had just missed photographing the 'N' in lovely winter light, which he has never forgotten – for that reason I thought it kinder not to include the picture this time! Another notable cross-country line was of course the Somerset & Dorset, and this section includes a shot taken at Templecombe shed one summer evening showing a selection of the line's motive power resting after their day's exertion. Visiting Templecombe today it is difficult to believe how busy a junction it was, but a least the 'rationalised' station on the main Salisbury to Exeter line remains open.

Wales was an area rich in long secondary and cross-country routes such as the remote 56-mile-long line from Carmarthen to Aberystwyth, the Mid Wales line and the scenic route along the Cambrian Coast, all of which feature in the section. Given the sparse services on these lines, private transport was essential to sample them all, which could easily cover a week or more. During my tours round the principality, many was the soaking I endured in the changeable Welsh weather, especially in the days before I changed my scooter for a car. But at least you could always turn wet weather to your advantage, as I think the picture on page 58 shows. Much further north, this section finishes with two pictures taken at Kyle of Lochalsh in the days when it was far less accessible than it is now.

Bourne End: '1400' 0-4-2T No 1421, 11 March 1961
Although this picture is not technically perfect, as I had to make a long hand-held exposure due to the restricted amount of light available, it does capture the atmosphere of a small station at night.

Ashurst: 'H' 0-4-4T No 31278, 17 March 1962
Ashurst in steam days was a delightful station situated on the border of Kent and Sussex. Apart from trains through to Uckfield and beyond, it was served by a regular service from Oxted to Tunbridge Wells West worked by vintage 'M7' and 'H' Class locomotives. Push-and-pull-fitted No 31278 looks a little tired but makes a splendid picture leaving the station for Tunbridge Wells West.

Left **Rowfant: 'M7' 0-4-4T No 30052**
Alison and I were captivated by Rowfant station, the building having a 'Hansel and Gretel' quality about it. We wondered if it could be turned into an attractive home, but this was not to be. In February 2008 the building was still there. The 'M7' is arriving with a push-and-pull set comprising ex-LSWR coaches on a train from Three Bridges to East Grinstead.

Below **Rowfant: 'M7' 0-4-4T No 30378**
On a then quiet road past the station, two girls out on a bicycle ride wait at the level crossing gates for the 'M7' to pass, which is propelling its train to Three Bridges.

Above **Grove Tunnel, Tunbridge Wells: 'H' 0-4-4T No 31544**
Some of the trains from Oxted ran through to Tunbridge Wells Central and Tonbridge. Here No 31544 has just emerged from the 187-yard-long Grove Tunnel shortly before joining the main line from Hastings at Grove Junction.

Right **Dorking North: 'E4' 0-6-2T No 32470, 17 December 1960**
The 'E4s' were among the many vintage locomotive types that could be seen at work on the Southern Region in the 1950s and early 1960s. Included in their duties were Christmas parcel trains like this one from Bricklayers Arms to Horsham, which has paused at the station on this cold morning.

Above **Cranleigh: 'M7' 0-4-4Ts Nos 30050 and 30129**
Push-and-pull trains between Guildford and Horsham were generally booked to cross at Cranleigh, an attractive station almost midway along the line. No 30050 is propelling its train to Horsham, as denoted by the lamp over the buffer beam.

Below **Brighton: 'M7' 0-4-4T No 30049, 19 August 1955**
Complimentary to the Guildford to Horsham service was that from Horsham to Brighton, which was regularly worked by 'M7s'. The noise of the steam from the safety valves of Horsham shed's No 30049 echoes round the arched roof of the station as the locomotive waits to leave for its home town.

Right **Bramley & Wonersh: 'Q1' 0-6-0 No 33001**
Guildford shed occasionally used a 'Q1' on the Guildford to Horsham line trains and sometimes they could also be seen travelling over this route on Sunday excursion workings to the South Coast. On a normal service train No 33001 is leaving the station for Cranleigh and Horsham. Just visible is the station's W. H. Smith & Son shop by the level crossing.

Below **Reigate: 'N' 2-6-0 No 31815**
The footbridge over the line at the west end of the station was always a good vantage point to photograph trains going in the Guildford direction such as this one with the 'N' hauling two Hastings-gauge corridor coaches. The signal box and level crossing are still there, but with today's heavy traffic the passage of a train can cause long tailbacks on the A217 road at peak times.

Left **Between Riddlesdown and Upper Warlingham: '4MT' 2-6-4T No 42088**
Before the advent of the Standard 2-6-4Ts, the LMR Fairburn tanks were in charge of many of the trains on the Oxted line. No 42088 is coming over Riddlesdown Viaduct spanning the big chalk quarry situated on the dip slope of the North Downs, with a train for Brighton via Oxted, Eridge and Lewes.

Below **Oxted Tunnel: '4MT' 2-6-4T No 80015**
I imagine that it would now be impossible to take a photograph in this location, given the growth of lineside vegetation since the days of steam. Working a train to Tunbridge Wells West, No 80015 has just emerged from the 1 mile 501 yard tunnel under the North Downs and will be picking up a little speed before stopping at Oxted.

West Hoathly: '4MT' 2-6-4T No 80152 Lewes: 'C2X' No 32440, 28 December 1956

In *Thanks for the Memory* I finished with two pictures of the Lewes to East Grinstead line, and here are a couple more as a reminder of its last days. The Standard tank is leaving the station for East Grinstead in a heavy snowstorm in the winter of 1957/58. The building behind the locomotive is the Bluebell Inn, which has now been converted to a private residence. At Lewes the double-domed 'C2X' has just arrived with a one-coach train from East Grinstead.

Above **St Leonard's shed: 'A1X' 0-6-0 No 32636, 'Q1' 0-6-0 No 33036 and 'N' 2-6-0 31401**
Not many photographs seem to have been published of St Leonard's shed, which was located close to West Marina station, and I took this one from a local train to Hastings. The 'Terrier' is displaying duty '413' on its white disc, which shows that it has been used on the Kent & East Sussex line freight working from Robertsbridge to Tenterden. No 32636 makes an interesting contrast with the utilitarian lines of the 'Q1'.

Left **Guildford shed: '0415' 4-4-2T No 30582, 19 March 1961**
The Railway Enthusiasts Club at Farnborough ran some excellent special trains with unusual motive power in the 1950s and early 1960s, such as the 'LSWR Suburban' railtour. The '0415' worked the train from Waterloo and back via Staines, Windsor, Woking, Guildford and Leatherhead, and is receiving some well-deserved attention at the shed before the return leg of the journey.

Between Gomshall and Dorking Town: 'V' 4-4-0 No 30915 *Brighton*, 23 July 1960 Summer Saturdays saw a number of extra trains over the Reading to Redhill line, notably the through service from Wolverhampton to Brighton, Hastings and the East Kent resorts such as Folkestone and Sandwich. As can be seen from the change in gradient towards the rear of this through train, the 'Schools' has just breasted the long climb from Chilworth and can ease off down the 1 in 96 gradient towards Dorking. Sadly the lovely iron bridge has now gone, replaced by a modern concrete structure.

Above **Ryde St John's: 'O2' 0-4-4T No W33 *Bembridge***
The delightful Victorian character of the railways in the Isle of Wight is evident in this picture of No W33 leaving with a train for Newport and Cowes. Standing in the bay platform adjacent to the fine signal gantry is No W22 *Brading*.

Left **Near Smallbrook Junction: 'O2' No W35 *Freshwater***
No W35, with its short freight train bound for Medina Wharf, makes a delightful sight on this spring day as it approaches the junction on the Cowes line. As this photograph was taken out of the main holiday season, the double-track section between Smallbrook and Ryde St John's is being worked as two single lines, the other one being used for Shanklin and Ventnor trains.

Right **St Kew Highway: 'T9' 4-4-0 No 30715**
This romantically named station was still quite a remote spot when I took this picture one summer evening in 1958. The 'T9' is coasting in with a train for Okehampton and will pass 'West Country' No 34029 *Lundy* on one for Padstow.

Below **Camelford: 'U1' 2-6-0 No 31903**
More usually seen in Kent, but displaced by electrification, a few 'U1s' were tried out on the North Cornwall line in 1961 to replace the 'T9s', which were worn out. However, they were not liked and went back east. Highlighted by the setting sun the locomotive is setting off towards Okehampton with a lightweight train brought up at the rear by an ex-LMS six-wheel gangwayed passenger brake-van.

Chilcompton Tunnel: '2P' 4-4-0 No 40696 and '7F' S&D 2-8-0

We are on one of our regular summer Saturday visits to the Somerset & Dorset line. This classic pairing makes a fine picture as the locomotives struggle out of the tunnel on the climb up to Masbury summit. Judging by the amount of Gresley stock in the train, it is probably the celebrated Cleethorpes to Sidmouth and Exmouth service.

Above **Near Masbury: '7F' S&D 2-8-0 No 53807**
Early on a warm summer evening, near the end of a busy day of photography on the line, the '7F' is climbing towards Masbury with a northbound stopping train consisting of a Gresley coach and a Maunsell set.

Below **Templecombe shed: 1958**
A line of locomotives, including two S&D 2-8-0s, a '2P' 4-4-0 and two '3F' 0-6-0s, rest after their day's exertions. The tiny single-platform Somerset & Dorset Templecombe station can just be seen in the background through the smoke.

Above **Cheddar: '5700' 0-6-0PT No 9771**
Working a train from Yatton to Witham, the Pannier tank pauses at the attractive Brunel overall-roofed station. The wide space between the tracks belies the fact that this was once part of the broad gauge.

Below **Chard Central: '4500' 2-6-2T No 5522**
The design of the station at Chard Central was similar to Wells though scaled down to suit the single-track line. On this sunny evening the '4500', which will have come in from Taunton, is waiting to leave for the short 3-mile run to Chard Junction.

Tiverton: '1400' 0-4-2T Nos 1420 and 1470, September 1961
Tiverton was served not only by trains to and from Tiverton Junction on the main line but also on the Exe Valley line from Exeter to Dulverton. Watched by the signalman in the fine GWR box, No 1420 is leaving for Dulverton while a Pannier tank rests in the bay platform between shunting duties. Meanwhile in the station No 1470 is waiting to propel its train south to Exeter. It is perhaps worth mentioning that Tiverton Museum is home to an almost forgotten '14XX' 0-4-2T, No 1442.

Above **Talyllyn Junction: '5700' 0-6-0PT No 3661**
This station was a delightful spot, the junction for the lines northwards to Three Cocks Junction and south to Talybont and Torpantau. On this very wet day No 3661 is about to go into the tunnel as it pulls out of the station past the fine GWR lower-quadrant signal, bound for Brecon.

Left **Trawsfynydd: '7400' 0-6-0PT No 7414**
In the autumn of 1958 I was staying with an aunt and uncle in a farmhouse near Beddgelert and, not having any transport of my own, persuaded them to drive me over to Blaenau Ffestiniog so I could have a ride on the line to Bala and take some photographs. The line wound its lonely way over the moors, reaching a height of 1,278 feet above sea level at Cwm Prysor, with Trawsfynydd as the principal intermediate station.

Between Dryslwyn and Golden Grove: '7400' 0-6-0PT No 7439
It was very pleasing to be able to photograph this train from Carmarthen to Llandeilo in sight of Dryslwyn Castle, after which 'Castle' No 7018 was named. The River Tywi can be seen in the background skirting the rocky bluff on which the castle stands.

Sugar Loaf, Central Wales line: Standard '5MT' 4-6-0
On this glorious summer day in 1963 Alison and I are on the A483 road looking down on the Central Wales line. We are using our crash helmets to hold the bilberries we are collecting on the hillside, but I have to break off to photograph the Standard 'Class 5' climbing the gradient towards Sugar Loaf Tunnel with a train from Swansea Victoria. In the distance are the Cambrian Mountains.

Sugar Loaf Summit: '5MT' 4-6-0 No 45406; '4MT' 2-6-4T No 42388
Up at the summit the 'Class 5' is about to enter Sugar Loaf Tunnel on the descent to Llandeilo, while at the signal box itself Alison took this picture of the Fowler tank in charge of another train to Swansea, with the crew handing over the single-line token to the signalman.

Fairbourne: '3MT' 2-6-2T No 82000 and '4300' 2-6-0

As is so often the case in West Wales it is a pouring wet day and I have taken shelter at the station. However, all is not lost photographically as the edge of the platform canopy makes a nice frame for this photograph of the two locomotives sweeping in with a train for Barmouth.

Above **Trevor: '5700' 0-6-2T No 4683**
In contrast to the predominantly rural nature of the line from Barmouth to Ruabon, it was always a surprise that over the last 2 miles from Trevor it ran though industrial surroundings, home to Monsanto Chemicals. On this wet day the locomotive is arriving at the station with an eastbound train.

Below **Strata Florida: '4300' 2-6-0 No 7321**
I always wanted to take some pictures at the evocatively named 'Strata Florida' station situated near the Cistercian abbey of the same name. This was not that easy as there were only three trains in each direction on weekdays over the 56-mile-long line from Aberystwyth to Carmarthen. However, I have made it to the station to picture the 'Mogul' arriving with a train from Carmarthen.

Near Welshpool: 'Manor' 4-6-0 No 7903 *Barcote Manor*

Shrewsbury shed took pride in turning out a beautifully prepared 'Manor' for the 'Cambrian Coast Express'. No 7903 displays whitened buffers and smokebox door fittings as it heads across the River Severn at Cilcewydd with the westbound train.

Near Llandre: '2251' 0-6-0 No 2268
The morning sun is still quite low in the sky, but just high enough the illuminate the wheels of this Collett 0-6-0, which makes a fine sight climbing the 1 in 75 gradient towards Llandre with a train from Machynlleth to Aberystwyth.

Green Bank Halt: '2MT' 2-6-2T
Tucked away in a deep valley, the obscure Green Bank Halt was served by trains on the line between Wellington and Much Wenlock. However, the service was never going to be a commercial success since trains took about three-quarters of an hour to do the 11 miles, with 11 stops! The Ivatt 2-6-2T is waiting at the halt with an afternoon service from Much Wenlock while the guard looks out in vain for any sign of passengers.

Above **Between Dunstable Town and Luton Bute Street: '2MT' 2-6-2T No 84004, 30 March 1961**
On this clear early spring day I found this good vantage point on the aptly named Blow's Downs to photograph the push-and-pull train from Dunstable to Luton climbing the steep gradient up the escarpment. The line closed in 1965.

Below **Peplow: '2MT' 2-6-2T No 41204**
Typical of the light local trains worked by the Standard and Ivatt 2-6-2Ts is this service from Crewe to Wellington, which is just arriving at the station. What a lovely tranquil summer evening it is, and neat rows of wheat sheaves in the large field behind the station are a very rare sight nowadays.

Burscough Junction: '3MT' 2-6-2T No 40199, January 1958

It is a sunny but cold morning at Burscough Junction station. I imagine that the smartly dressed young lad waiting on the platform with his Mum is going shopping at Preston in this train hauled by one of the 1938-built Stanier locomotives.

Ashey: 'O2' 0-4-4T No W33 *Bembridge*, August 1965
Thanks to the efforts of the Isle of Wight Steam Railway, trains still operate through Ashey station. In this pleasant scene taken one fine summer afternoon *Bembridge* is arriving at the single platform with a train for Ryde Pier Head.

Near Gomshall: 'U' 2-6-0 No 31799, Saturday 2 January 1965
This was the weekend that marked the end of steam working on the Reading to Redhill line. It was a clear sunny day ideal for winter photography as can be seen in this picture of 'U' class No 31799 on the 1 in 100 climb between Chilworth and Gomshall with a train for Redhill.

Langstone Bridge: 'A1X' 0-6-0T, 6 November 1963
This beautiful photograph taken by Alison has been reproduced several times before but I make no apology for taking the opportunity of using it again. Like many other enthusiasts, Alison and I went down to Hampshire for the last day of the Havant to Hayling Island branch. On this still autumn afternoon, as the sun set, we stood on the main road bridge to the east of the line as the 'Terrier' made for Havant.

Near Bala: Standard '4MT' 4-6-0
To my mind this is an almost perfect railway photographic location – high up on a steep hillside Alison took this picture of a Dolgelly to Ruabon train near Bala hauled by a '75000' Standard '4MT' 4-6-0. Once again I took the black and white version, which I messed up by getting the locomotive mixed up with a telegraph pole!

Woodburn: 'J27' 0-6-0 No 65861

Much further north in the breezy open Border country of Northumberland, South Blyth shed's 'J27' 0-6-0 No 65861 is shunting wagons in the station on the weekly goods train from Morpeth. The Cheviot Hills can be seen in the far distance.

Near Warrington: '5MT' 4-6-0
A very cold frosty morning sees the 4-6-0 climbing towards the big girder bridge over the Manchester Ship Canal with a semi-fast train for the north.

Patricroft shed: '8F' 2-8-0 No 48549
Nothing in preservation can recreate the atmosphere of the steam shed, typified here with the '8F' resting amidst shafts of sunlight at Patricroft shed, Manchester, in 1967.

Near Leslie: 'J38' 0-6-0 No 65914
Working a freight train from Thornton Junction and Markinch, the 'J38' is crossing the viaduct carrying the Leslie branch over the River Leven.

Warrington Bank Quay Low Level: '2MT' 2-6-2T No 41217

In the hard winter of 1961/62 a local train for Manchester Oxford Road leaves the Low Level station past the prosaically named 'Slutchers Lane' signal box. In early 2008 the nearby Arpley Junction signal box still survived in use. Passenger services were withdrawn from the Low Level station in September 1962.

Glasgow Queen Street Low Level: 'V1' 2-6-2Ts

I have come down from the High Level station and have been lucky enough to secure this sunshine-and-shadow picture in the smoky depths of the Low Level. One locomotive is waiting to leave with a train on the North Clyde line while the other comes in under the signal box, which can just be seen through the smoke. The pleasing arrangement of the platform barrows was quite by chance!

Kyle of Lochalsh: '5MT' 4-6-0s Nos 45476, 44722 and 44798, summer 1959

I know this is a familiar view of Kyle station but, given the fine weather and the amount of interesting detail it contains, I thought it worth including. With the mountains of Skye dominating the background, the 'Class 5' waits to leave for Dingwall and Inverness. Meanwhile at the small two-road shed two more 'Class 5s' await their next turns of duty.

Branch lines

I think I have to say that I probably derived more pleasure from photographing bucolic branch lines than any other, so it was fortunate that both the Southern and especially the Western Regions inherited a wealth of these lines, many of which were located quite near to me in the steam era. Their attraction was perhaps compounded by the ever-present threat of closure, so nearly all the branches depicted in this section are no longer with us. In contrast, the areas covered by the other three Regions of British Railways had comparatively few true branches since railway construction in the formative years of the 19th century had concentrated on the development of main and through lines.

However, I start this section with two of the branches the London Midland Region did operate, Foxfield to Coniston in the Lake District and Wolverton to Newport Pagnell. One of my favourite branches in the South of England was Paddock Wood to Hawkhurst, a delightful rural byway running through orchards, hop fields and woods. Little remains to be seen of the branch though the knowledgeable motorist on the busy A262 road might glimpse a small section of 'railway' fencing where it crosses the course of the line adjacent to the site of Goudhurst station. One of the branches that has survived is from Brockenhurst to Lymington, currently served by 'heritage' electric multiple units, while the one-time Swanage branch is operated in part by the Swanage Railway. Further to the west no selection of branch pictures would be complete without including the superb Axminster to Lyme Regis line, one of the finest anywhere, I suggest. The counties served by the Western Region were rich in branch lines, some of which have survived into the preservation era, such as part of the Watlington branch as far as Chinnor and the Dart Valley Railway in Devon from Totnes Riverside to Buckfastleigh. Many of the ubiquitous but charming '14XX' 0-4-4Ts worked Western Region branches, such as those to Windsor & Eton Central, Fairford, Abingdon and Fowey, among others.

While I was sorry to have just missed photographing the Highland 0-4-4Ts on the Dornoch branch in Scotland, there was the compensation of seeing Western Region tank locomotives at work on mixed trains on the branch and at the opposite end of the country, as depicted on page 86. In the Highlands the branch to Killin, though short, was a delightfully scenic one and I was fortunate to capture the happy everyday scene at the station, as seen on page 88.

Below **Coniston: 1957**
On this very overcast day in the autumn of 1957 there are no passengers to be seen under the overall roof at the terminus. The station's appealing chalet style of design and the mountains looming up in the background give an almost Swiss feel to the scene. A push-and-pull train in the charge of Ivatt 2-6-2T No 41221 is waiting to leave for Foxfield.

Opposite **Newport Pagnell branch: '2MT' 2-6-2T No 84002**
This 4-mile-long branch ran from the West Coast main line at Wolverton to the Buckinghamshire market town of Newport Pagnell, and was served by some six trains each way on weekdays only. In the upper picture No 84002 is working its push-and-pull train by the windmill near Bradwell, and later is seen after arrival at Newport Pagnell. The branch closed to passenger traffic in December 1961 and now forms part of a cycle way.

Above **Allhallows on Sea: 'H' 0-4-4T No 31193, 1 August 1960**
I always enjoyed visits to the Allhallows branch, which was set amid the bleak marshlands of North Kent. As is well known, the Southern Railway had ambitious plans for developing Allhallows as a holiday resort, but it was not to be. This picture of the 'H' waiting to leave for Gravesend conveys something of the desolate and windswept character of the area.

Left **New Romney & Littlestone-On-Sea: 'H' 0-4-4T No 31295**
Equally as windswept and perhaps more remote than Allhallows was the branch from Appledore to New Romney. The 'H' has just arrived with an evening train composed of LSWR and LB&SCR coaches, nicely lit by the low sun.

Folkestone Harbour: '5700' 0-6-0PTs, 3 June 1961
The motor cycle combinations, rarely seen nowadays in everyday use, are almost as interesting as the Pannier tank-hauled boat train, which is leaving the harbour to start the assault of the 1 in 30/36 gradient up to the main line at Folkestone Junction. Steam-hauled special trains still occasionally run down the branch, though it is now singled and seems unlikely to hang on for much longer.

Goudhurst: 'H' 0-4-4T No 31530 and 'C' 0-6-0 No 31259, 12 June 1961
My brother and I have got up early and travelled down from New Malden on my Lambretta LI 125 scooter to be in time to see the first trains of the day crossing at Goudhurst at about 7.55am. Despite this being the last day of services, there are few people about on this sunny morning. The 'C' is arriving bound for Paddock Wood, while the 'H' will continue to Hawkhurst.

Between Paddock Wood and Goudhurst: 'H' 0-4-4T No 31308, 31 May 1961
Leaving Goudhurst: 'C' 0-6-0 No 31588, 12 June 1961
Such was the charm of the Hawkhurst branch that I could not resist two more pictures, one showing the 'H' coming through the hop fields past the Goudhurst Distant signal, and the other of the 'C' leaving the station for Hawkhurst with a specially strengthened train on the last day.

Above **Lymington Pier: '4MT' 2-6-4T No 80134**
The fireman of the Standard tank is working the ground frame at the Pier station to allow the locomotive to run round its train. In the misty distance across the Solent are the hills of the Isle of Wight.

Below **Lymington Town: 'M7' 0-4-4T No 30053**
Before the arrival of the Standard' tanks the branch line was worked by 'M7s'. No 30053, which was destined to spend some time in the United States after its withdrawal, coasts into the Town station with a train for Brockenhurst. The proximity of the attractive harbour always made this area a 'must' for photography.

Swanage branch: 'M7' 0-4-4T No 30108

I first visited the Swanage branch in 1950 on holiday with my parents. The branch must have made a big impression on me because I spent quite a lot of the time at the terminus watching the trains on the bridge by the small single-road shed. Apart from the use of more modern push-and-pull coaches, little had changed over the intervening years when I took these pictures in 1961 of No 30108 on the outskirts of the town en route for Wareham and approaching Worgret Junction along the long straight from Furzebrook with the Purbeck Hills behind.

Above **Seaton branch: 'M7' 0-4-4T No 30667**
The Seaton and Lyme Regis branches were very different in character. The latter followed a steep and tortuous path into the hills from Axminster, while the former mostly ran along the lush valleys of the rivers Coly and Axe. Between Colyford and Colyton, passing meadows near the River Coly, the Seaton Junction-bound 'M7' is hauling a Urie 'Ironclad' push-and-pull set.

Below **Lyme Regis branch: '0415' 4-4-2T No 30583**
At Combpyne there is an ex-LSWR Camping Coach to be seen in the siding as the Adams tank pulls away from the single platform for Lyme Regis.

Above **Between Bude and Whitstone & Bridgerule: 'T9' 4-4-0 No 30338**
In the early 1960s contrasting types of locomotive could be seen at work on the Bude branch. The elegant 'T9' makes a fine sight accelerating away from Bude at East Trelay with a typical North Cornwall line train of the day.

Right **Whitstone & Bridgerule: '3MT' 2-6-2T No 82018**
No 82018, built in 1952, arrives at the station bound for Halwill Junction. The vintage station nameboard is especially fine, with blue lettering on a white background.

Bodmin North and Wadebridge: 'O2' 0-4-4T No 30199, September 1961
When I was young places like Bodmin and Wadebridge, home of the fabled Beattie 'Well tanks', seemed impossibly far away, emphasised by the long column of evocative place names that were shown in Table 50, 'WATERLOO to THE WEST OF ENGLAND', of the Southern Region's green-bound timetable. Sadly, all traces of the station at Bodmin North have gone, but Bodmin Jail, which can be seen in the background of the picture, is still there, though now a restaurant. No 30199 is preparing to run round its train. At Wadebridge the same locomotive is leaving with a train for Bodmin North while, on the left, Beattie 'Well tank' No 30586 is on station pilot duty.

Right **Callington: 'O2' 0-4-4T No 30225**
As on the Bude branch, more modern motive was drafted into Cornwall to work the steeply graded line from Bere Alston to Callington. At the latter station in 1958 the old order still holds sway as the 'O2' blows off steam noisily waiting to leave the delightful station with a train for Bere Alston.

Below **Gunnislake: '2MT' 2-6-2T No 41316**
A couple of years later the Ivatt 2-6-2Ts are at work on the branch, typified by No 41316, which has just arrived at Gunnislake with a train from Bere Alston. What a wonderful old car it is to the left of the train – a pre-war Austin, perhaps?

Eynsham: '5700' 0-6-0PT No 9653
This picture shows a scene that at the time seemed as if it would be there for ever. In the summer of 1960 two trains are passing at Eynsham on the Fairford branch. The driver of the Ford Anglia car and his passenger wait patiently at the level crossing for No 9653 to leave for Oxford, maybe giving them time to admire the well-planted station garden.

Right **Welford Park: '5700' 0-6-0PT No 4609**
Perhaps the neat little Ford saloon in the small parking bay belongs to the railwayman on the platform. The Pannier tank has just arrived from Newbury and will soon continue its journey to Lambourne.

Below **Lambourne: '2251' 0-6-0 No 2221**
At the terminus the Collett 0-6-0 is propelling its train into the single platform. The new-looking horse box in the siding is a reminder of the importance of this area for racehorse training.

Near Golant Halt: '1400' 0-4-2T No 1419

Of the several branches off the Plymouth to Penzance main line, the short one to Fowey was one of the most pleasant. On its 15-minute journey from Lostwithiel, the 0-4-2T is running alongside the wide River Fowey, giving its passengers an unrivalled view over the water.

Abingdon: '1400' 0-4-2T No 1435
Windsor & Eton Central: '1400' 0-4-2T No 1436
Two branches in the Home Counties worked by the useful little 0-4-2Ts were Radley to Abingdon and Slough to Windsor & Eton Central. Both branches were just over 2 miles long and enjoyed a frequent service of push-and-pull trains. A very dirty No 1435 rests in the platform at Abingdon, while at Windsor No 1436 is propelling its train into the station, which is overlooked by the impressive ramparts of Windsor Castle.

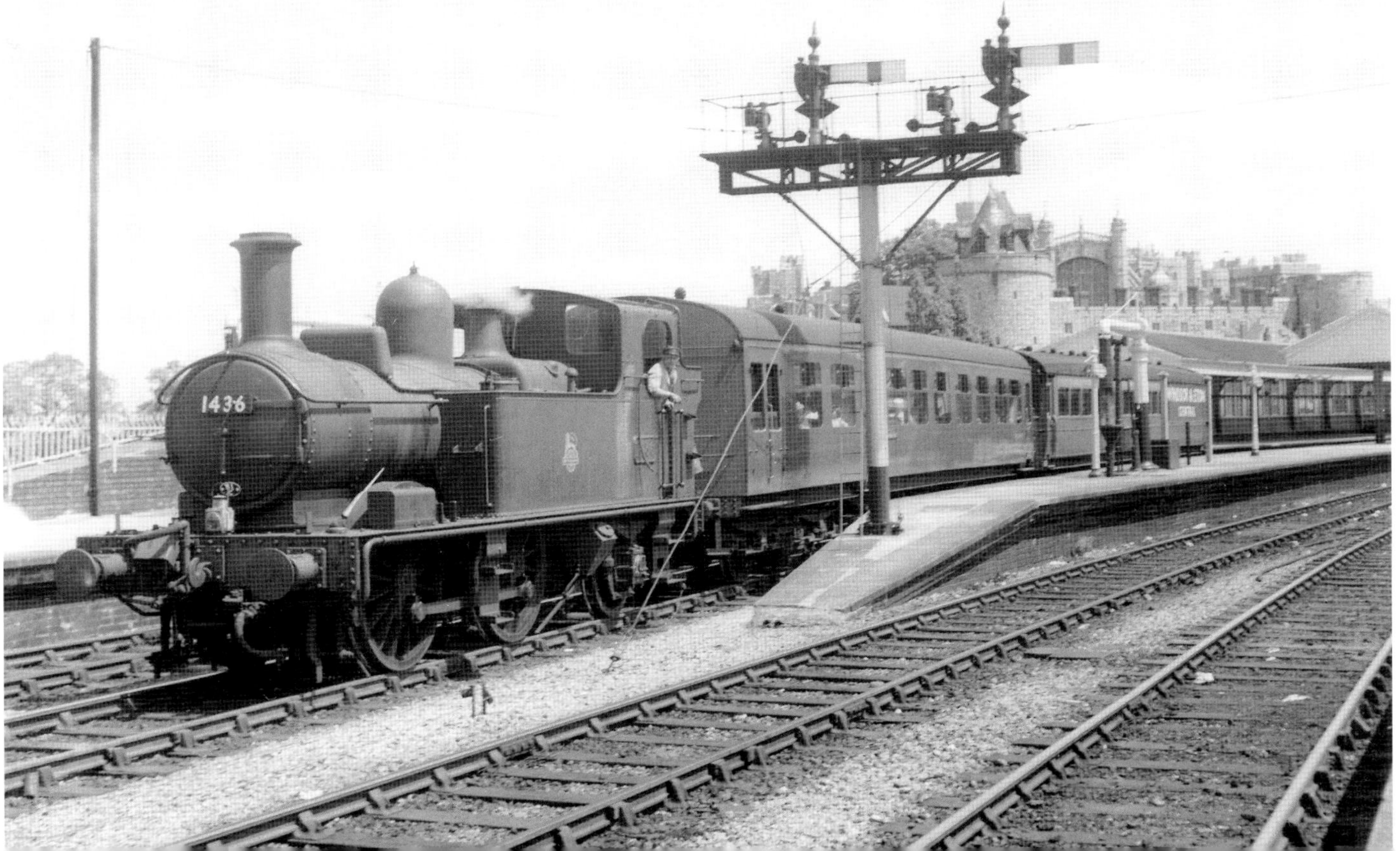

Near Avonwick: '4500' 2-6-2T No 4561, Easter Monday 1960

My friend Gerry Siviour, who has just photographed this Kingsbridge to Brent train, is standing on the little bridge spanning the fast-flowing River Avon. Some of the locations on this line were very reminiscent of those on the Ashburton branch, which followed the River Dart for much of its course.

Above **Totnes: '1400' 0-4-2T No 1466**
Like No 4561, No 1466 has survived into preservation and can still be seen on the Dart Valley line. Here the locomotive is coasting into the down main line platform at Totnes with a train from Ashburton.

Right **Between Coombe Junction and Liskeard: '4500' 2-6-2T No 5557, April 1960**
On this fine spring day the 2-6-2T is climbing the gradient towards the main line with a train from Looe and will shortly go under the lofty Moorswater Viaduct before running into Liskeard.

Left **Near Nancegollan: '4500' 2-6-2T No 4568**
Down in the far west of Cornwall, the Helston branch was notable for running mixed trains. The scenery in this picture is quite reminiscent of the west of Ireland, where such trains were more common. No 4568 is just to the south of Nancegollan where it will cross a train bound for Helston.

Below **The Mound: '1600' 0-6-0PT No 1649**
More than 700 miles away from west Cornwall in Scotland, mixed trains could also be found on The Mound to Dornoch branch, where some '1600' Class Pannier tanks had been exiled to replace the Highland 0-4-4Ts that previously worked the line. The train is leaving The Mound station in the summer of 1959 with the waters of Loch Fleet behind. The line closed a year later in 1960.

Above **Elgin: '4MT' 2-6-0 No 76105**
No 76105 was built at Doncaster in 1957, so was almost new when I took this picture of it at Elgin in 1959. It was first allocated to Kittybrewster shed (61A) and was regularly employed on trains on the branch to Lossiemouth.

Below **Ballinluig: '2P' 0-4-4T No 55218**
Of much older vintage was this 1913-built ex-Caledonian Railway locomotive, which ended its days on the branch to Aberfeldy, closed to passenger traffic in 1965. Hopefully the train will pick up some passengers from a connecting service on the main Perth to Inverness line.

Killin: '2P' 0-4-4T No 55173, 29 July 1961
There is quite a little gathering of Mums and their children at Killin station before No 55173 sets out on its 4-mile journey to Killin Junction in the summer of 1961. The design of the ladies' dresses and shoes is typical of the time.

Above right **Between Killin and Killin Junction: '2P' 0-4-4T No 55173, 29 July 1961**
Amid fine Highland scenery this train has just left Killin on the 15-minute or so journey along Glen Dochart to the junction.

Right **Loch Tay shed: '2P' 0-4-4T No 55230**
A mile or so further on from Killin was the small locomotive shed at Loch Tay. The Killin to Loch Tay section was closed to passengers in 1939 but the shed was retained for the use of the locomotives working the branch.

Freight workings

What an astonishing variety of freight trains there were to photograph in steam days! This final section shows them on main, secondary and branch lines all over the country. Most freight trains now are of the bulk-load variety worked largely by the impressive Class 66 diesel locomotives, far removed from the old-fashioned steam-operated mixed goods. Unlike today the motive power used on freight trains could produce some surprises, for even though they were still at work on a main line, there was something sad but fascinating about seeing one-time top-link passenger locomotives demoted to hauling freight trains. The pictures of No 30850 *Lord Nelson* on page 91 and 'Jubilee' No 45629 passing Moore on page 114 illustrate this. However, some freight trains were important enough to warrant special front-line motive power such as the beautifully turned-out 'V2' on the down 'Scotch Goods' shown on page 112.

While photographers in the steam era had passenger train timetables to refer to, access to internal working timetables was required to glean details of goods trains, so photographing them was generally a bit hit-and-miss. However, the uncertainty about the movement of these trains gave a sense of achievement when a pleasing photograph of one was secured. Some lines were of course goods-only, like the famous Wenford Bridge branch depicted on page 92, where even a few photographs made the long journey to the West Country worthwhile. The lovely but remote line to Woodburn in Northumberland, seen in the colour section of this book, could also produce some fine material, especially as the train could quite easily be followed if you were fortunate enough to have a car. Freight trains abounded elsewhere in Northumberland on the gritty mineral lines centred around North and South Blyth, a very different world for those railway photographers from the 'soft' south who were more used to homely pick-up goods trains carrying out leisurely shunting at delightful country stations.

In contrast to a rural branch or secondary line, which might have one goods working a day at the most, some lines were extremely busy. A prime example was the GN/GE Joint line running north from March in Cambridgeshire. I remember a visit there in 1960 when even on a Saturday one train followed another in both directions worked by a wide range of locomotives including a Stanier 2-6-0. Some pictures of the line appear in this section and I particularly like the one of the 'B16/3' crossing Twenty Foot Drain on its way north, which appears on page 108. At the other end of the scale I suppose one of my most lucky pictures was of the elusive Garsdale to Hawes goods train on page 120. Even in 1958, when I took the picture, this area was not nearly as accessible as it is now and, had I possessed a car, I don't think I could have driven it over the high moorland roads in such snowy weather. Still, as occasionally happens for the railway photographer it was a case of being in the right place at the right time.

Shepherds: '4500' 2-6-2T No 5537, 8 September 1958
Shepherds was a delightfully named station on the Newquay to Chacewater and Truro line, which lost its passenger service in 1963. Other stations with memorable names on the branch were the 'two Goons', Goonbell Halt and Goonhaven Halt. As a change from the usual '4500'-hauled passenger train, No 5537 is leaving the station with a pick-up goods.

Right **Ashford (Kent): 'D1' 4-4-0 No 31739 and 'C' 0-6-0 No 31589, May 1961**
The 'D1' has just arrived at the station with the 7.24am train from London Bridge while the 'C' passes with a freight from the Hastings line. The third rail is in place ready for the commissioning of the second phase of the South Eastern electrification.

Below **Wimbledon: 'Lord Nelson' 4-6-0 No 30850 *Lord Nelson***
Over on the Western Section main line the sight of a 'Lord Nelson' on a freight train was not all that common, even towards the end of their life. In the summer of 1959 *Lord Nelson*, in very smart condition, is on the working that left Nine Elms goods depot just before 8pm for Basingstoke and Southampton Docks, often loading to 50 or more short-wheelbase wagons. The lineside path on the left of the picture was a splendid location to watch the trains, but unfortunately the view has now been spoiled by the erection of tall prison-like security fencing.

Wenford Bridge branch: '0298' 2-4-0T No 30585, April 1960
The Wenford Bridge branch was among the most photogenic in the country and how lucky Gerry Siviour, my brother and I were with the weather for our visit. The backlighting has dramatised this picture of No 30585 as the wheels of its train squeal round the sharp curve on the approach to the china clay depot. Thanks to the efforts of the Bodmin & Wadebridge Railway and other benefactors, we can still enjoy the sight of an '0298' at work in the area.

Right **Larks Barrow cutting: 'U' 2-6-0 No 31794**
On the Didcot, Newbury & Southampton (DNS) line between Litchfield and Whitchurch, the 'U' is heading south through this wonderfully named and picturesque chalk cutting, with a tank train for Fawley.

Below **Leaving Bude: 'N' 2-6-0 No 31835**
'N' Class locomotives were long associated with the Southern lines west of Exeter, both on passenger and freight trains. No 31835, which looks as if has had a general overhaul recently, is slowly pulling away from the North Cornwall resort with this freight train, which contains six empty coal wagons.

Between Charlbury and Ascott-under-Wychwood: '2800' 2-8-0 No 2894, 6 April 1963

Near Chipping Campden Tunnel: 'Hall' 4-6-0 No 5945 *Leckhampton Hall*, 21 July 1961

I eagerly looked forward to the freight trains that interspersed the regular 'Castle'-hauled expresses on the Oxford to Worcester line, since they would invariably produce some good photographs. No 2894 is plodding north with a train of coal, while the 'Hall' is working hard up the 1 in 100 gradient from Honeybourne towards the tunnel.

Near King's Sutton: '5100' 2-6-2T No 4118, 15 July 1961
Preserved main-line steam can still sometimes be photographed at this spot to the north of King's Sutton, but I doubt whether the lineside is as clear as it was in 1961 when I took this picture of a train of iron ore.

Ruabon: 'Castle' 4-6-0 No 5063 *Earl Baldwin* and '1600' 0-6-0PT No 1632

I was so intent on photographing the 'Castle' at the head of this train from Chester to Shrewsbury that I only just turned round in time to see the Pannier tank approaching. The attractive vintage GWR lower-quadrant signals greatly add to the scene.

Above **Charlbury troughs: '5700' 0-6-0PT No 3750, 24 June 1961**
These next two pictures illustrate the versatility of these useful locomotives. No 3750 has just reached Charlbury troughs en route to Oxford with what looks like two freight trains combined, and I am intrigued to know what the second vehicle from the locomotive is, but I am told it could be a weighing-machine van.

Below **Parkend: '5700' 0-6-0PT No 3609**
At Parkend, on the section of the line from Lydney recently re-opened by the Dean Forest Railway, the Pannier tank is marshalling its freight train before travelling south. Note the Midland Railway-pattern signal by the locomotive.

Between Llanfyllin and Bryngwyn: '2MT' 2-6-0 No 46522
I had stayed the night in Welshpool and was making my way towards North Wales, but stopped off at the Llanfyllin branch, where I photographed what was surely an archetypal rural branch-line freight train amidst the pleasant surroundings of the Welsh Border country.

Above **Llanfyllin: '2MT' 2-6-0 Nos 46509 and 46522**
I had earlier seen the Ivatt 'Mogul' shunting wagons at Llanfyllin before it left for Llanymynech. The lovely old wooden Cambrian signal is 'off' ready for the departure of the branch-line train hauled by sister locomotive No 46509, which will precede the goods.

Below **Burwell: '2MT' 2-6-0 No 46469**
The versatile Ivatt 'Moguls' were widely distributed around the country, as shown here by No 46469, which has paused at Burwell with a short freight train from Mildenhall. It has crossed the main Ely to Newmarket line at Fordham.

Shugborough Tunnel: '8F' 2-8-0 No 48036

I always enjoyed photographing trains around tunnels, particularly on the London Midland Region, which erected attractive and informative nameboards like those seen in the picture. With the need to avoid delaying express passenger trains over this double-track section of the West Coast main line, the '8F' is hurrying south.

Chipping Campden Tunnel: 'Modified Hall' No 6994 *Baggrave Hall*
The exhaust from a 'Castle', which has just passed with a train for Oxford, is billowing out of the tunnel, and the white steam sets off the Worcester-bound 'Hall' very nicely as it enters the half-mile-long bore on a falling gradient of 1 in 100.

Approaching Fairbourne: '2251' 0-6-0

The Collett 0-6-0 and its single-wagon load are dwarfed by the majestic panorama of the Barmouth Estuary. I am driving north on the Lambretta and it looks as though once I get going again, I will have to crouch down behind its screen to try to avoid a soaking as a heavy rainstorm is coming in from the sea.

Near Drws-y-Nant: '4300' 2-6-0 No 7341

On this fine summer evening the sound of No 7341 coming up the long climb from Dolgelly with an eastbound freight train could be heard from some way off. The mountains of the Cader Idris range dominate the background.

Winslow: 'Jubilee' 4-6-0 No 45584 *North West Frontier*
A long line of surplus wagons are in the sidings as No 45584 passes the station with a westbound freight train.

Above **Hednesford: 'G2A' 0-8-0 No 49377**
The 'G2A' looks unusually smart as it carries out some shunting of coal wagons in the sidings adjacent to the station.

Below **Stanbridgeford: 'G2A' 0-8-0**
The old LNWR locomotive has stopped to shunt some wagons with a pick-up freight from Luton to Leighton Buzzard. I remember that the station was in a terrible condition, like the paintwork on the 'G2A', which was so bad that the legend 'LMS' can just be discerned on the tender.

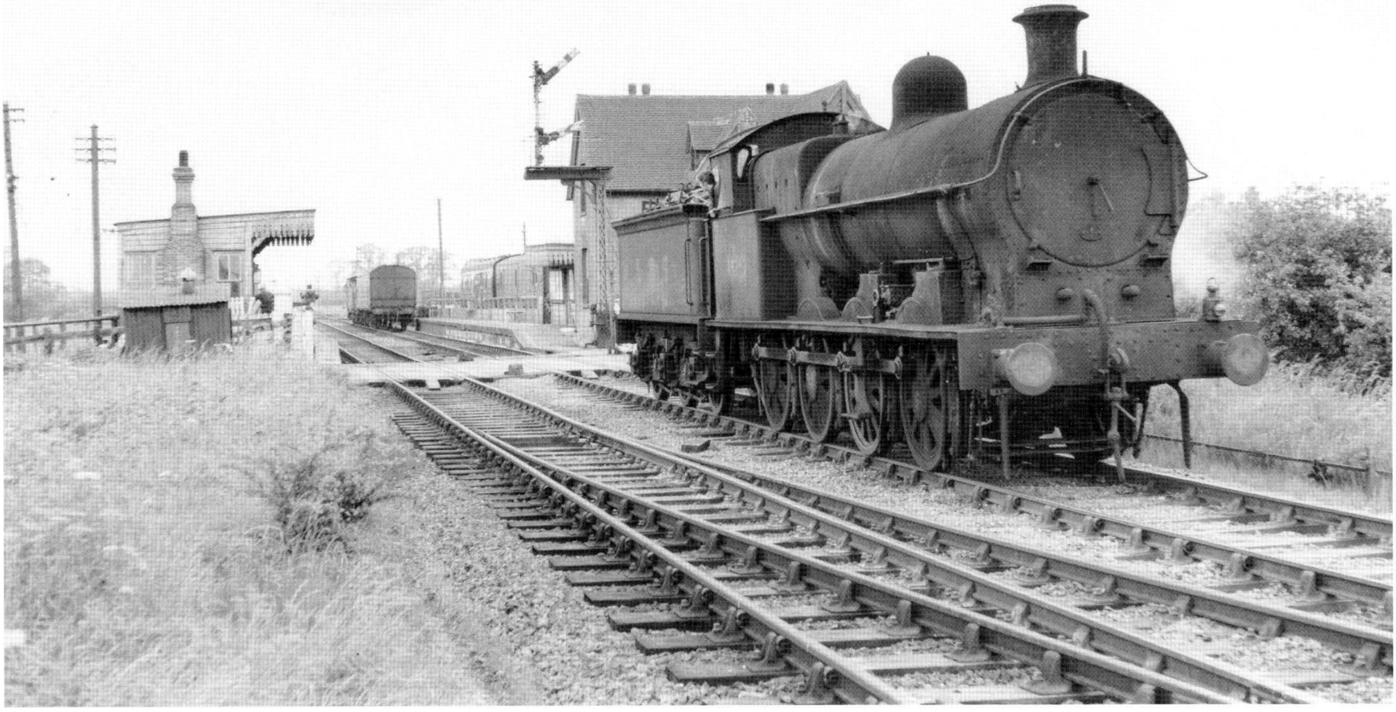

Blackwell: '9400' 0-6-0PT No 8400

More often seen banking at the rear of a train, the big Pannier tank is the train engine and is straining to reach the top of the Lickey Incline with this long freight, possibly of repaired wagons from Bromsgrove Wagon Shops. Its progress is so slow that it looks as if the local children on the footpath will be able to overtake it.

Blackwell: '5MT' 4-6-0 No 44857; '4F' 0-6-0 No 44045 and '9400' 0-6-0PT No 8400

The 'Class 5' has just started the descent of the Lickey with a vans train from the Birmingham direction. The beginning of the change in gradient from 1 in 291 at Blackwell station to the 1 in 37¾ of the incline can be seen at the third van back from the locomotive. From the same direction the '4F' is beginning a cautious descent of the incline with a loaded coal train.

Leaving Whitemoor Yard, March: 'B16/3' 4-6-0 No 61464

In the early 1960s the GN/GE Joint line running north from March towards Spalding was very busy with freight traffic even on a Saturday, when this picture was taken. The locomotive is easing northwards out of the yard past Twenty Foot Drain.

Cowbit: 'O4/3' 2-8-0 No 63666
French Drove for Gedney Hill: 'B1' 4-6-0 No 61083
Here are two more pictures on the Spalding to March line. The Retford (36E)-shedded 'O4/3' is bringing its train slowly southwards from the Nottinghamshire coalfields past Cowbit's impressive-looking goods shed. The 'B1' is handling a similar load, probably destined for power stations.

Keadby Lifting Bridge, Althorpe: 'B1' 4-6-0 No 61021 *Reitbok*

I am on the east side of the River Trent and have been lucky enough to capture an eastbound freight hauled by a clean named 'B1' crossing the bridge. After I took this picture I jumped in the car and was able to secure another shot of the train as it climbed the steep bank towards Scunthorpe.

North Blyth: 'K1' 2-6-0 No 62022 and 'J27' 0-6-0 No 65880, 14 June 1965
Bordering the North Sea, North Blyth featured extensive sidings for the nearby large coal-fired power station. The 'J27' is arriving with a loaded coal train from Ashington. Against the backdrop of the power station's four chimneys, which were demolished in 2003, the 'K1' is leaving the yard with return empties.

Welwyn South Tunnel: 'V2' 2-6-2 No 60903
The sparkling condition of this 'V2' is a credit to King's Cross shed and reflects the importance attached to express freight workings like this afternoon 'Scotch Goods' heading north up the East Coast main line.

Above **Welwyn Viaduct: '9F' 2-10-0, 6 August 1960**
Designed by William Cubitt and opened in 1850, this 40-arch, 1,560-foot-long viaduct spans the valley of the River Mimram. Perhaps with a modern wide-angle lens I could have included more arches, but his picture from the west side still gives some sense of the impressive nature of the structure.

Right **North of Berkhamsted: '7MT' 'Britannia' 4-6-2 No 70021** ***Morning Star***
This 'Britannia' has been recently transferred from the Western Region to the London Midland Region shed at Willesden and looks well cared for, still retaining its nameplates. Putting out a fine exhaust, accentuated by the cold north-west wind, it heads towards Rugby and Crewe on a fast freight train. The impressive telegraph pole route on both sides of the line typifies the West Coast route in steam days.

Near Moore: '6P' 'Jubilee' 4-6-0 No 45629 *Straits Settlements*

The sun is low in the sky on this clear, cold frosty morning. I am at one of my favourite locations to the south of the bridge over the Manchester Ship Canal to picture the 'Jubilee' heading towards Crewe. Luckily for me the wind is from the east, rather than the more usual west, keeping the exhaust clear of the train.

Above **Winwick: '7P' 'Britannia' 4-6-2**
My son Richard is well wrapped up against the cold as he watches the 'Britannia' heading north out of Warrington with a long vans train. As I mentioned in *Thanks for the Memory*, this area was still agricultural land in the mid-1960s but has now been built on as the town has expanded.

Below **Warrington: '5MT' 4-6-0 and '9F' 2-10-0**
These trains have just crossed the River Mersey, which can be seen on the right of the picture. The 'Class 5' is on its way out of the sidings at Arpley, while the '9F' is heading south on the main line to Crewe.

Left **Daresbury: '9F' 2-10-0**
The very cold winter of 1962/63 produced some wonderful conditions for photography, as here at closed Daresbury station. The '9F' is heading into the mist towards Chester past the frost-covered platforms.

Above **Oxenholme: '9F' 2-10-0**
As was so often the case in that part of the country, it is pouring with rain, but the wet stone flags on the platform give this picture tremendous atmosphere. It was in these conditions that black and white photography came into its own, for I think the same scene in colour would not have had the same impact.

Right **Warrington Bank Quay: '6P' 'Jubilee' 4-6-0 No 45586** ***Mysore***
In the icy winter of 1962/63 the 'Jubilee' has come to a stand in the down main line platform with a parcels train for the north. The lights are already on in the signal box on this day of leaden sky and freezing fog, but at least the snow is brightening up the scene a little.

Near Miller's Dale: '8F' 2-8-0 No 48711

This picture gives a good idea of the classic limestone scenery that could have been enjoyed today had the Manchester to Derby line remained open. Hauling a mixed freight, the '8F' is cautiously heading down the gradient from Peak Forest towards Matlock on a continuous descent of some 20 miles.

Crosby Garrett: '5MT' 4-6-0

The sweeping vistas on the Settle & Carlisle line were in complete contrast to the deep valleys on the Midland Railway route through the Peak District. This freight is heading south up the 1 in 100 gradient towards Ais Gill summit – on the extreme right of the picture is the unmistakable outline of Wild Boar Fell.

Hawes: '4F' 0-6-0, 23 January 1958
I related in the caption on page 89 of *Thanks for the Memory* how I had made a trip in the winter by train to this Wensleydale town. Having a little time to spare I walked out along the road to Garsdale and was in the right place to take this picture of the local goods running down from the main line looking for all the world like an O-gauge tin-plate train in the snowy landscape. The tender cab on the '4F' will be giving the crew some additional protection from the cold.

Shap: ‘5MT’ 4-6-0

Rather than being close to the line, as was the temptation when taking pictures on Shap, I have walked back at Greenholme to show the glorious panorama of the fells, unsullied in those days by the M6. The ‘Class 5’ is on a long train of banana vans from Garston, Liverpool, and is assisted in the rear by a 2-6-4T.

Above **Kirkby Stephen: '4MT' 4-6-0 No 75019**
Beneath a lowering sky threatening rain, the small 4-6-0 has steam to spare as it races down the 1 in 100 gradient towards the station with a lightweight northbound freight working.

Left **Kirkby Stephen East: '4MT' 2-6-0 No 43106**
Over at the East station, which lost its passenger service in 1962, the Ivatt 'Mogul' is shunting some wagons. Little is left of the once extensive facilities and the Darlington-bound track through the attractive overall-roofed station has been lifted. However, the Stainmore Railway Company is making efforts to re-open the line to Appleby East. The locomotive spent some of its career on the Midland & Great Northern line and retains its tablet-catching apparatus on the tender. It was withdrawn in June 1968 but happily has survived into preservation and is currently being overhauled.

Above **Greenodd: '2F' 0-6-0 No 58182, 3 August 1961**
The little Johnson 0-6-0 is coasting into the station with a pick-up goods from Haverthwaite and has just crossed the substantial bridge carrying the line over the River Leven. Unfortunately this attractive southern section of the branch to Windermere Lakeside has not survived, but at least steam can still be seen up the road at Haverthwaite.

Below **Meldon (Northumberland): 'J27' 0-6-0 No 65861**
We are following the once-weekly goods from Morpeth to Woodburn and here it is bustling through this remote wayside station. The main event was of course the return working, chimney-first, which is featured on page V of the colour section.

Falahill: 'A3' 4-6-2 No 60068 *Sir Visto*, 31 July 1961
Near Stow: 'B1' 4-6-0 No 61359, 31 July 1961
My brother and I are on our way back from Scotland and are pleased to have been able to photograph these 'Waverley' line freight trains on the climb to Falahill summit and near Stow.

Invergordon: '3F' 0-6-0 No 57575
The '3F' is approaching the station from the south with a local goods working and the driver is preparing to hand over the single-line token to the signalman. The waters of the Cromarty Firth can be seen in the background and the fuel storage tank is a reminder of Invergordon's importance as a naval base.

Crianlarich Lower: '5MT' 4-6-0 No 45487
Up in the Highlands in 1959, the 3,582-foot-high Ben More dominates the scene as the 'Class 5' runs into the station with a freight for the Oban line.

Near Annfield Plain: '9F' 2-10-0 No 92098, 15 June 1965
This '9F' was one of the locomotives fitted with air pumps to operate the side doors of the 56-ton bogie tippler wagons used on the heavy iron ore trains between Tyne Dock and the steelworks at Consett, which closed in 1980. With a train of these wagons the '9F' is about to pass a North Eastern Railway slotted-post Distant signal. Finally an appropriate picture to finish showing one of the iron ore trains heading away towards Consett up the 1 in 50 gradient.

Index

Roman numerals indicate the colour pages.